Snapshots

Glimpses of My Family in 1930's & 1940's America

Stories Compiled by Brenda Hill

Format, Layout, and Design by Cynthia Hill

Copyright © 2007 by Brenda Hill and Cynthia Hill. All rights reserved. No part of this book may be used or reproduced in any manner without written permission of the publisher.

Printed in the United States of America.

ISBN: 978-0-6151-4816-8

Cover Art by Cynthia Hill

Published using the services of Lulu
To purchase additional copies, please visit
www.Lulu.com

Dedication

I would like to dedicate this book to my mother and my daughter, who are great inspirations to me.

I would also like to dedicate this book to those who have electricity, indoor bathrooms, televisions, computers, cars and compact discs. There was a time when none of these existed.

Table of Contents

Grandpa & Grandma	5
Mom's Memories Begin	9
Background	11
Clayton Place	13
Melrose	15
Catlettsburg	18
Gilkerson Branch	21
Prichard	23
Buffalo Creek	25
Friends	30
School	35
Holidays	41
World War II	44
Boyfriends	46
Neighbors and Friends	50
Earl	54
Crime and Punishment	58
Leisure	60
This and That	64
Baltimore	70
Reflections	72

***Note:** Any terms appearing in this text in bold print can be found, along with their definitions, in a small glossary in the back of this book.

Grandpa & Grandma

Into simple and quiet times in the hills of Narrows, Virginia, my grandfather Charlie Wiley was born in 1892. He was one of thirteen children.

He and his brothers and sisters grew up to lead difficult but interesting lives and they had challenging experiences. Grandpa's brother, Dennis, became a coal miner in the mines of West Virginia. His brother, Tom, was an electrician in the mines. Another of his brothers, Woodrow, worked and died in the mines. He was killed in a machinery accident when he was in his thirties.

Charlie's brother Russell served in World War I and developed serious lung problems from inhaling poison gas during the war. Yet another of my grandfather's brothers, Garfield, was blown up and burned inside a tank while serving in World War II. He survived, however, the explosion nearly burned his stomach away and Garfield lived largely on goat's milk from then on. His ears were also burned away. Even though sophisticated plastic surgery didn't exist in those days, surgeons were able to reconstruct his ears and Garfield lived a relatively normal life from then on.

My grandfather Charlie grew into a tall, handsome man with curly black hair. He was outgoing, friendly and generous. He tried working in the mines for a brief time as his brothers had done, but he really didn't like the work.

My grandmother, Jessie Mae Adkins, was born in the hills of Kentucky in 1900. She was one of six children. Their lives, like those of my grandfather's family, were challenging and there were many memorable moments. Grandma enjoyed recalling a particular instance from her youth. Their family had heard through the grapevine that someone with a car was visiting nearby. Everyone in the vicinity hurried to the site so they could have the experience of seeing a "real car". This provided some novelty and excitement for their otherwise quiet community.

My grandma Jessie grew into a beautiful, black haired young woman.

Charlie and Jessie met and married in 1917. The years passed and they were blessed with five children who brightened their lives.

Each baby was born at home, with a doctor in attendance. The children are listed in order of their birth.

Dorothy Mae	Born in Columbus, Ohio
Catherine Louise	Born in South Carolina
Earl William	Born in Virginia
Betty Marie	Born on Mayo Trail, Louisa, Kentucky
Billy Lee	Born in Melrose, Kentucky

Betty Marie is my mother and she has shared many of her fond memories with me. How wonderful it is to relive her experiences and imagine being in her early homes.

As the family grew, my grandfather Charlie worked with his brother-in-law Slim Easton, building bridges for a while. They worked in various locations and Jessie and the children moved with him from place to place. The family had several homes.

Grandpa worked in the **shipyards** in Baltimore, Maryland and he also painted houses for a living.

I wish my grandfather had been more interested in attending church. He was, however, interested in God's Word and one of his favorite pastimes was sitting outside and reading his Bible.

Grandpa didn't drive a car, and we really don't know why. This was rather unusual for a man of those days, especially since automobiles were quickly becoming so popular.

Grandpa was a big kidder and a prankster. He liked to tease. He was good-hearted. He was the type of person who would be willing to give his last dollar away to help someone who might need it.

People were always welcome in my grandparents' home. Even though there was always much to do, the pace was slow and easy. Grandpa liked people, was always happy to see visitors, and readily welcomed them. There was never an inconvenient time for people to drop by and visit.

Grandma was a hard worker. She was serious, but easy to talk to whenever one of the children had a problem. My grandmother was very tough when she felt someone was not doing the right thing. She canned vegetables, baked bread, cooked for the family and hoed corn.

She made **sassafras tea**. She milked the cow. She didn't own a washer and dryer. Instead, she washed the family's laundry on a **washboard** and hung it to dry from a clothesline in the yard. My grandmother worked in the garden and walked miles to the store to buy necessary groceries and other items. She primarily bought staples like flour, salt, corn meal, sugar, coffee, vinegar, cloth and thread. Her family was her only luxury. She didn't have the opportunity to go to the hair salon, get her nails done or wear makeup. Her life was demanding and not glamorous. She met her tasks head-on and didn't flinch.

My mother jokes when she says, "Our family was so poor, we never knew there was a **Depression**". For them, nothing was any different after the 1929 **Stock Market Crash** than it had been before. They had very little before 1929 and very little afterwards.

My Grandparents

Mom's Memories Begin

Time and distance have a way of changing things, yet memories remain vivid and clear in my mother's mind just as if it were still the 1930's and 1940's in Kentucky and West Virginia. The snapshots are clear and focused, yet the world was very different from today.

Mom's Only Baby Picture

Background

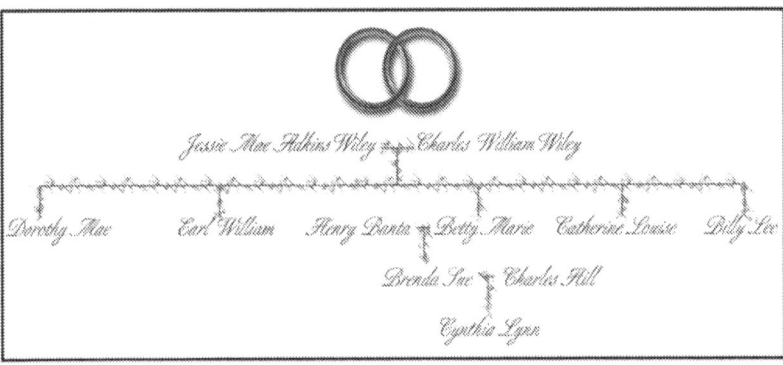

Clayton Place

My mother's earliest memories are from Clayton Place. Mom was very young at this time and her memories from here are vague and limited. The family rented a farmhouse in this rural area from a farm owner known as "old lady Clayton" who lived just down the road from them. On one occasion, a family passed through Clayton Place on their way to Virginia, and while they were there, they offered my mother a dog. My grandmother allowed her to keep it. The dog was little and white with curly hair and Mom named the dog Poodle for obvious reasons.

In those days and times, school kids were permitted to take their smaller brothers and sisters to school with them occasionally. One such time, my Aunt Dorothy took Mom, who was probably three or four years old at the time, with her and their brother Earl, to class. Mom recalls some of the older boys picking on Earl and threatening to hurt him. She remembers starting to cry. She also remembers her loyal pleading with those boys not to hurt her "Bub-oh", as she fondly referred to him.

Melrose

Melrose was a small village which had one church and no businesses. The village was set between a river on one side and the railroad tracks on the other. It was a town of 200 to 300 people. The village was very scenic and "cute", reminding my mother of a fairy tale. Mom lived here when she was four to six years old. She was still very young and, again, her memories are few and brief. The family kept no livestock here, nor did they have a garden. However, many other families in the community had gardens or farmed. They grew potatoes, tomatoes, corn and other crops. When corn is cut down in the fall, it is cut off at an angle. On one occasion, Mom managed to fall on a cut-off cornstalk as she ran through a cornfield here. The corn stalk ran up underneath her kneecap, and provided an unpleasant memory of those days.

Bill

The doctor came to the Wiley home in Melrose when Earl was nine years old and Mom was only four years old. A baby was about to be born and Earl and Mom were asked to go upstairs. They waited with eager anticipation. Time passed and eventually a voice shouted up the stairs to tell them that it was a boy. My grandparents named him Billy Lee Wiley.

Earl, who already had three sisters to put up with, was delighted. He jumped up and down on the bed and yelled, "I've got a brother to play with! I've got a brother to play with!"

Someone else in the house was not quite so happy about the event, however. That someone was Mom's little dog, Poodle. My grandmother was the primary caregiver for Poodle and the dog came to love her a lot. Poodle came over to the bed where Grandma lay with baby Billy beside her, front paws on the bed so he could see. Shortly thereafter, the dog disappeared and was never seen again. The family thought it might have been a case of jealousy.

The Doll

When my mom was about five years old, Grandpa brought her what she believes may have been her first doll. She remembers that when my grandpa first brought it home to her, he hid it under his coat. The doll's head was made from something similar to plaster. She loved the doll and played with it a lot. Apparently, she didn't watch the doll as closely as she should have. Once she left it on the porch and when she returned, she found that someone had hammered the eyes out of the doll. Almost certainly the culprit was her brother Earl. The behavior pretty well fit his profile, but she never really knew for sure. Some time later she forgot the doll out in the yard and the dew further ruined it.

Hobos

Hobos were tramps or vagrants - the homeless of those days. Hobos were commonplace and often hopped the trains to travel from place to place. They often came to the back doors of homes in Melrose, asking for a meal. Grandma always complied.

Mom's picture from primer class (the equivalent of today's kindergarten)
Can you see the safety pin?

Catlettsburg

Catlettsburg was the biggest of the towns the Wileys lived in when their children were young. Catlettsburg is a river town and here they lived in a big house. Their back yard faced a field. Behind that field was a very high hill and a path ran up that hill to a cemetery. Mom was a first grader at this time. Here they had no garden or livestock. There were many businesses in Cattlettsburg and the Wileys remained here until about 1935. Mom has only a few recollections of this place.

Bullies

Children can be sweet, innocent and sometimes gullible. Mom was no exception. When she was a first grader, one of the boys came up to her and looked at her as if he saw something wrong. He asked her what was in her mouth. She opened her mouth, only to have him throw sand into it.

The bullying gene apparently ran in that boy's family. At a later time, Mom was walking home from school with his sister. The girl was much older and a good deal bigger than my mother. She suggested stopping at the service station on the way home to go to the restroom and Mom followed. When they got into the restroom, the girl blocked the door and wouldn't let my mother leave. She somehow took Mom's shoes from her, put them in the sink and filled them with water. My mother finally threatened to tell her sister, Louise, and her brother, Earl, what had happened. The girl then decided to leave her alone.

Pig-Girl

No rural area has ever existed without a few legends. One of the stories told by the young people of this community regarded an incident where some of them walked by a neighbor's house one evening and, through a window, observed the girl who lived there. She was looking into a mirror. It was told that the girl had the face of a pig. Everyone knew the girl had been born with some deformities. For a long time a "pig tale", which rumored the girl to be half pig and half human, circulated throughout the area.

Teeth

Mom remembers a booklet the children were given in first grade to help them learn about teeth. The teeth were drawn cartoon style, with cute faces and expressions. The booklets belonged to the school. When it was time to move from Catlettsburg, Mom didn't want to move because she didn't want to leave her tooth booklet behind.

Gilkerson Branch

This was a rural, desolate area with perpetually muddy roads. It is my mother's least favorite home. One rather unusual experience here stands out in her memories:

The Tenant

One day when Mom was about six or seven years old, Grandpa went to the train depot in the nearby town of Prichard. While he was in one of the grocery stores there, a stranger walked in. The man was handsome and fairly young, and his name was George Grogan. Grandpa was always friendly and never knew a stranger. He and this gentleman began to talk and it turned out that the man was looking for a place to rent.

Grandpa and Grandma had a small building at the back of their house which was similar to a **smokehouse**. A deal was made for George to rent the back building. He had a few pieces of furniture which he moved into the building. He walked to get his groceries. He led a very quiet life and stayed in a lot. He didn't bother anyone.

Two sisters lived down the road from my grandparents and they became aware of the presence of this handsome man. Both were married, but were undeterred with regard to their interest in this man. The husband of one of the sisters traveled a great deal. This gave the woman the opportunity to start sending her little son down to the small building, carrying notes from his mother to George. The women's pursuit of George became his undoing. Eventually, the women did something which made George mad. George took a gun with him to where the women lived and a skirmish developed. Aunt Dorothy and Uncle Earl were visiting the women at the time. No one was hurt, and my family was never sure of exactly what had happened.

After this unwelcome attention was drawn to him, George moved away, seeming to flee the area.

My family never knew for certain what George's story was, but it was told that the FBI later picked him up. As time passed, it was rumored that George Grogan was a member of **Al Capone**'s gang from Chicago. I guess we will never know for sure.

Prichard

My mother's family moved to Prichard when she was about seven years old. This was where Grandma's parents lived.

The Quarter

One day, Mom and Aunt Louise were walking to their grandfather's house when Mom looked down and discovered a piece of paper folded up, near the railroad tracks. It had a quarter in it. After Louise and Mom briefly squabbled over the huge find, Mom kept it. She thought she was rich, but even as a child Mom was frugal. She went to the grocery store and purchased items she thought were most needed and most practical. From a young age, she was never one to waste money. With this money she purchased a dozen eggs for 12 cents, a tablet she needed for school, and perhaps another item.

Louise

Buffalo Creek

If you follow Spring Valley Road and Route 60 for twelve miles or so out of Huntington, West Virginia, you will arrive in Buffalo Creek. It was here that the Wileys lived next. They moved here when Mom was nine years old and over the years they lived in three different homes. They lived about three miles from the elementary school, which was a one-room schoolhouse called Stoney Point School. The junior high school and high school were combined and they were the home of the "Buffalo Bisons". This was my mother's favorite home. Time dragged occasionally in this rural area, but Mom has fond memories of these days. It was in Buffalo that my family lived for several years and here that the children "grew up". Mom's memories from here are vivid and plentiful. It was a wonderful time. As Mom refers to it, it was "the most fun place". She says that the poor times were the best times.

Life in Buffalo

In Buffalo, the family lived in three different places. All five children were still at home when they lived in the first two houses. Here they had two dogs named Sparky and Don.

In the mountains there were hot days, but rarely a hot night. The nights were cool and one always needed covers. They had a fireplace and the family kept rocks on the **hearth**. Often, they would put a warm rock into their beds at night to warm the bed before bedtime. They enjoyed the "luxurious" facilities of an **outhouse**. For quite a while, they had no electricity here. They had chickens, two pigs and a cow.

A stove sat in the kitchen which used coal and wood. In one side of the stove was a tank which they filled with water. The water warmed there would become their source of hot water.

It was Earl's and Mom's job to bring in wood and coal supplies for the day. Earl would chop the wood and Mom would gather kindling wood. They fed the chickens and slopped their two pigs which they kept for meat. The pigs they kept grew very large (to about 500 pounds). The family gathered eggs each day as well. My grandmother milked their cow and sometimes Bill would help her. Mom wasn't very proficient in the milking process.

The cow slept in the barn at night and in the morning was let out to the pasture. Each evening it was someone's job to go get the cow and bring her home. When it was Mom's turn to bring the cow home, she came up with a "great" idea. Sometimes she would swat the cow to make her move faster. Then Mom grabbed onto her tail for a ride. Looking back on this adventure, she later realized this may not have been the greatest way to treat an animal.

Periodically, the cow became "lonely". She was in heat and would moan and make an awful racket until Grandpa took her to a bull in the vicinity for a "date".

When they got hungry for poultry, one of the members of the family would simply shoot one of their chickens. At other times, they might just cut the chicken's head off. After this process, the chicken would often run around for a few moments and then fall over. (Hence the expression, "running around like a chicken with it's' head chopped off".) Mom never had the nerve to kill a chicken as most of the rest of the family did. She was too tender-hearted to do that. The next step in preparation was to scald the chicken in hot water and pluck the feathers. Then they simply cut up the bird and cooked it.

Grandpa was in charge of butchering the hogs, which is a pretty gruesome ordeal. The process took about a day.

Earl and Mom gathered blackberries and raspberries for my grandmother. Grandma made jelly and jam from them. Mom and my uncle sold some of the berries to make money. The blackberries were sold for 20 cents a gallon and the raspberries were sold for 30 cents a gallon. Raspberries were not nearly as plentiful as blackberries were. Earl and Mom split the money.

The young entrepreneurs made money in other ways as well. Earl and Mom sold garden seeds, Cloverine Salve and Redbud Salve door-to-door. Earl sold GRIT newspapers and Mom tagged along with him.

Since times were hard they tried to save their money. On one occasion, their older sister Louise wanted a new dress and asked them for the money. She told them she would help them to earn it back, so

Earl and Mom gave her the money they had worked all summer for to buy the dress. Louise really loved that dress. By then, fall weather was moving in and some of the opportunities to earn money were dwindling for the winter. By the next spring the promise was forgotten and Louise never helped them earn more money.

Earl and Mom continued to try to save the money they made from their ventures. Mom was very frugal, but Earl spent much of his money on cigarettes and **Brilliantine** to keep his hair looking good for the girls. At one time when she was about ten years old, Mom had saved about $5.00, which was a great savings at that time. Grandpa happened to mention that if he had the money he would buy mash for the cow. Mash was a grain mixture fed to livestock. Mom gave him the money to buy the mash. As she recalls, it sold for about $5.00 per 100-pound bag. Grandpa could not believe she had saved that much money.

Another of Earl's and Mom's duties was to bring in water from the well each day. Their well was the old-fashioned kind with a rope, pulley and bucket. When bath time came, there was no hot and cold running water. They had to heat their water in the stove.

Mom and Aunt Louise took turns pouring warm water over each other's heads so they could wash their hair. In the early days, they used bar soap to wash their hair. Mom discovered shampoo when she was in her teens. The girls used rollers to style their hair. They often formed "pin curls" in their hair with bobby pins to create curly styles.

Grandpa cut Earl's and Bill's hair for them.

The girls had no sanitary napkins and had to use rags for this purpose. The family didn't have toilet tissue and used paper from catalogs instead. They didn't have toothpaste, so they brushed their teeth with baking soda.

Dorothy was able to get small amounts of makeup to use; primarily **rouge**, lipstick and face powder.

Grandma washed their laundry on a washboard, using lye soap.

They had a garden. They used to help with the spring planting by breaking up clods, fining up dirt and planting potatoes. There was always weeding and other ample work to do in the garden.

After Dorothy, Louise and Earl got married, the family moved to the third location. In this farmhouse they had a back-to-back fireplace between two big rooms. A grate opened into each room. One of these rooms was the living room and the other was Mom's bedroom. How cozy it must have been. At this home, they also had a wood stove, a well, a garden and animals to care for. Things here were very similar to their previous two Buffalo homes.

The Wileys

Earl Wiley

Friends

During my mother's journey to adulthood, she had three close friends. They liked to wade in the creek, play in the woods, chase boys, climb trees, swim in the "swimming hole" at the creek, play, and have fun. Occasionally one of the girls might spend the night at another's house. Mom remembers spending cold nights at Roberta's house. Roberta's mother would get a rock which had become hot from lying on the hearth, wrap it up and put it in the bed Mom was sleeping in, to help her stay warm.

Roberta and Mom liked to live dangerously. They often crawled under a fence where a bull was penned up and would tease the bull until he got mad enough to charge at them. Then they hurried to roll under the barbed wire fence just in time to escape before the bull reached them.

Mom and Roberta also enjoyed the sport of swinging from grapevines out into a nearby ravine. If their mothers had only known!

In their younger days, Ruby Hutchinson and Mom paired off with Lewis Stanley and Huffy Stevens. As they grew older and began dating, Beulah Stevens and Mom paired off with Menis Fraley and Huffy Stevens. Menis was not the most handsome, but he was a barrel of fun. Many liked to tease him and say that his name was really spelled "Menace".

Ruby

Ruby Hutchinson had a rather difficult life. She had two older brothers. Her mother died in childbirth when Ruby was only two years old. Her father Richard, lacking that mother's touch, felt inadequate to raise a daughter, particularly one of Ruby's young age. Ruby's Aunt Mary came to get her and she reared Ruby at her home much of the time. Mary's husband was a coal miner and they lived in the mining town of Lundale, West Virginia in Logan County.

The mines owned and operated company stores. The stores were similar to general stores and they sold clothing, groceries and gasoline. Miners were paid in paper certificates called scrip and these were only payable to the company stores for their merchandise. This was rather like bondage since the miners ended up paying all their "wages" back to the mining companies when they made purchases.

Miners' housing was simple and small. The houses were all alike, having the same size and shape and each were limited to about four rooms.

Ruby's Aunt Mary and her husband periodically had marital problems. It was at these times that Ruby went to live with her father, Richard, in Buffalo. Because of this shuffling back and forth between homes, she often had to switch schools in the middle of the school year, which made life harder for her. It was during the times that she lived with Richard that she attended school with my mom. She stayed with her dad more and more as she became older.

Mom dated Ruby's brother Wilford for a long time, but they eventually drifted apart.

Ruby married Newman Merritt at seventeen. They had two daughters. To this day, Mom and Ruby still correspond occasionally.

Ruby

Roberta

Roberta McCoy was a little older than Mom. She was a very pretty redhead and was very smart and rather flashy for those times. Mom and Roberta remained friends until Roberta grew up, got a job, married a handsome well-to-do Greek man named Paul Peleg. and moved to Huntington.

After couples were married in those days, they had what were referred to as "bellings", which were parties for the bride and groom. Roberta's and Paul's "belling" took place at her parents' home. Mom went to the event with Menis Fraley and Huffy Stevens. Guests teased the bride and groom until they were given candy and treats. Cow bells were rung and the guests played games. At this particular belling the guests played a game called Post Office. Boys and girls were separated into groups and each person was assigned a number. Then a player went into another room and called out a number. The lucky person whose number was called got to go into the room to get a kiss. By chance, the groom called out my mother's number. When she came into the room, Paul was careful to give her a **chaste** kiss on the forehead. As the game progressed, Huffy, who had liked Mom for a long time, caught on to which number was assigned to Mom. When Huffy entered that room, he called out Mom's number. She went to the room and he eagerly kissed her.

My mother later heard that Roberta and Paul had a daughter. At one point, their daughter was kidnapped, but they were able to get her back.

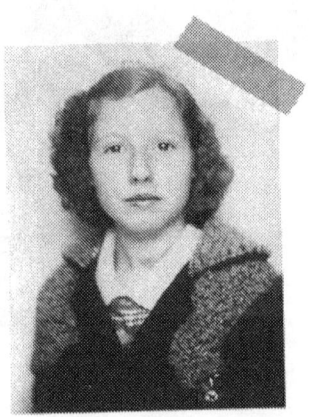

Roberta

Beulah

After Ruby and Roberta married their spouses, Mom became closer with another friend of theirs. Her name was Beulah Stevens. Beulah eventually married Ruby's brother Wilford and they had five children, one of whom later died.

Beulah

School

My mother went to elementary school in a one-room schoolhouse named Stoney Point School. It previously had two rooms, but one had been closed off for safety reasons. Six grades went to school there. Each grade sat in its' own row. Mom had to walk three miles to get there. She had a lot of fun walking to school, however. The children played as they travelled on their journey. The group grew larger as they got nearer to the school and more and more children joined them. As Mom neared the halfway point of her journey, they picked up the Staley children. It seemed they were rarely ready on time. This turned out to be a good thing, though, on cold winter mornings. On those terrible mornings, Mom and the other kids would go inside to get warm by the Staley's fireplace and wait on them to finish getting ready.

Boys wore pants or overalls to school. Girls always wore dresses. Many parents would never permit their daughters to wear pants, however, Mom and Roberta were allowed to wear pants for occasions other than school or church.

Mom was often made to wear not-so-nice-looking boots to school to keep her feet warm and dry. She didn't want the other kids to poke fun at her, so Mom made it a practice to take off her boots just down the road from their house, hide them in the bushes and not wear them to school. Each evening she picked them up, put them back on and wore them home.

In this rural area, everyone knew everyone else. Whenever someone in the area died, the school teacher would ask her class members if anyone wanted to attend the funeral. Mom and her friend Ruby liked school, however, they took far too many opportunities to go to funerals all over the place, just to get out of school. They thought it was a great way to have fun.

For holidays, the teacher would often use the name of the particular holiday as a challenge to the children to make as many words as possible from the letters in that holiday word. Mom always enjoyed doing this.

If the children were good, they got to stay after class and clean the blackboard as a reward. This provided a pleasant diversion from routine home chores and mundane activities that were a part of everyday life.

One year, Mom had a very young, female teacher. One of the big boys who had failed a couple of years did something wrong. The teacher tried to paddle him, but he took the paddle from her, and this made her cry.

The children were punished in other ways as well. Sometimes if someone misbehaved, the teacher drew a circle very high on the blackboard. The disobedient child had to stand on their tippy-toes and put their nose into that high circle for a long time until the teacher allowed him or her to stop.

The teacher often warned the children not to go near the creek when they were outside at lunch and recess. One winter day Mom, Lewis, Huffy and Ruby went to the creek anyway. The creek was iced over and Lewis walked out onto the ice. He broke through the surface, getting soaked in the process. The group returned to the school and naturally the teacher determined what had happened. The four all got paddled and Lewis sat by the coal and wood stove to dry out his clothes and warm himself.

The teacher also warned the children not to go into the room of the school which had been closed off. It was a dangerous place to be. So where did this obedient foursome go? To the other room, of course. They were climbing on the rafters and playing around in there when they were discovered by their teacher. Each received one swat with the paddle.

Neither the school nor the community had a library. Their teacher took it upon herself to borrow and bring a wooden case of books to the school each month for the children to borrow and read. She awarded certificates to the children each month to acknowledge the number of books they read during that period and to encourage them to read. Mom loved books. She remembers receiving a certificate one month for having read thirty-two books.

Mom's favorite books were "Heidi", "Tom Sawyer" and "Huckleberry Finn". She read each many, many times. She liked to dream and imagine having adventures like these children had. She envied Heidi and thought how great it would be to live in the Swiss Alps.

As fifth and sixth graders Mom and her best friend, Ruby, were permitted to teach the younger children and grade their papers.

The boys carried water from the nearest farmhouse and filled a bucket at the back of the room. There was a dipper in the bucket. Each child brought their own collapsible metal drinking cup, which they kept in their desk. When the children got thirsty, they filled their cups from the bucket.

The school was heated by a coal stove. Two boys were paid a small sum to be "janitors" and they brought coal for the stove in from the school yard.

Bill's lunchbox

Henry

Mom started out in school in the same grade as a boy named Henry Staley. Henry was a poor student, however, and failed two or three times. He was one of the school "janitors". Henry was paid a small sum to come to school early, sweep the floors and start a fire in the coal stove to warm up the one-room school building.

When mom was about ten years old, Grandma asked her to leave for school early one morning and deliver something to the home of a family friend who lived beyond the school. Mom decided to drop her books and things off at school before making her delivery. Henry was there working when she came in. The two were there alone. Henry started to pursue her and even though she was so young, she felt that something wasn't right. Perhaps his intentions weren't good. He began to approach her and she avoided him. It didn't take long, however, until he had her cornered. Not knowing what else to do, she threatened to tell her older brother, Earl. That's all it took for Henry to give up the pursuit.

Mom never told on Henry. She thought he already had enough problems to deal with.

The class of Stoneypoint School the year before Mom's arrival

Front Row: Ivory Lee Staley, Roberta McCoy, Carl Staley, Wilford Hutchinson, Sesco Maynard, Henry Staley, unknown
Second Row: Lewis Stanley, James Ward, Garrett Staley, Edmond Stanley, Huffy (Jennings) Stevens, unknown, Josephine Mays
Third Row: Loraine Ward, Kathryn Walters, Elizabeth Ward, unknown
Top Row: Elwood Hutchinson, Erma Lee Ward, Virginia Staley, Mildred Staley, Garnet Harmon

Holidays

Christmas

The Wileys lived in poverty and the children had very few toys. One year, Mom and Uncle Bill thought that they would have no Christmas presents, but their older sister Dorothy, came home with a beautiful, big baby doll wearing a glow-in-the-dark lace dress for Mom; and a big fire truck for Uncle Bill. The doll's head, hands and feet were made of a plaster-like material, and the rest was made from cloth and stuffed with straw. It had molded hair. Mom and her brother were thrilled with their gifts.

Every Christmas, they made their own decorations. They strung popcorn on string and they made rings out of construction paper and glued them together to make chains. They made ornaments from paper and wrapped aluminum foil around pine cones. Each child wrote their name on a shoe box. Grandpa put candy and fruit in the boxes once the children were asleep on Christmas Eve.

Mom's school presented Christmas plays each year as well. One year they performed "A Christmas Carol" complete with Tiny Tim. All of the children were supposed to say the last line of the play together, "God Bless us everyone". However Mom was one of the only ones to remember the line. The teacher remarked, "I can see who's been practicing".

Halloween

Every year at school for Halloween, they had a costume contest. It may come as no surprise that one particular year Mom had no costume. Grandma, however, had a pumpkin she had been growing. She dug out the insides and carved a face in it. Even though it was a little messy, Grandma placed the pumpkin on Mom's head. It made a great costume! Her teacher called her pumpkin-head and Mom won first prize for the contest.

Even though houses were widely spaced, the children went trick-or-treating, and played an occasional prank along the way. A neighbor owned a trailer which he used to haul things in. One Halloween, the kids released it and let it roll down the hill behind his house. On another occasion, they tipped over his outhouse.

Easter

Each Easter, the teachers held an Easter Egg Hunt at school. Each child would bring two colored eggs. All of the eggs were hidden by the teachers. The person who found the most eggs would win a prize —a nice Easter basket filled with candy.

As time went on, some of the older boys decided not to play fairly. They began to combine the eggs they found and claim that one of them found them all. In this manner, the older boys would sometimes win the basket and split the candy.

Mom's Sunday School teacher also had egg hunts for the children at her home. The children enjoyed snacks and had lots of fun together.

World War II

Mom's family had no electricity in Buffalo for a long time. They had no refrigerator or television. They kept food in the cellar to keep it cold. As time passed, they later got an **icebox** to keep their food cold. They burned wood and coal to stay warm. When Mom was thirteen years old, she and her family were listening to a battery-powered radio. It was December 7th, 1941. President Franklin D. Roosevelt announced over the radio that Pearl Harbor, Hawaii had been attacked by Japan. He told the people that the United States had declared war on Japan. This brought us into World War II. Aunt Dorothy's husband, Bill Rush, and Aunt Louise's husband, Walter Gillum, both later served in the military in this war. Mom proudly wore a pin practically everywhere she went which said, "Remember Pearl Harbor".

Mom's Pearl Harbor Pin commemorating the attack

Campaign buttons for Franklin Roosevelt and Harry Truman

Boyfriends

Clifford

Mom's first "boyfriend" was Clifford Wilson. Clifford was cute and ornery. He wore **knickers** much of the time. My mother was about nine or ten at the time and they often sat together in church. On one occasion, while hymns were being sung, he pulled Mom down onto his lap.

One evening, some older boys decided to play a prank by locking the church doors from the outside so that everyone would be trapped inside. The only way for people to get out of the church was through a window in the **foyer**. Clifford climbed out of the window and turned around to catch Mom as she crawled through the window.

Mom looked up to see her brother Earl standing there, giving her that special brotherly look that said "Betty's got a boyfriend". Earl laughed and Mom was truly embarrassed.

Clifford later moved away.

Huffy

Huffy Stevens liked Mom for a long time. Huffy had black hair. He was cute, sweet and fun. He used to bring her little gifts to show his love. One day when she was about ten years old, Mom and Huffy were walking through a field holding hands. Mom looked up and saw my grandmother walking down the road. Mom had been caught again.

When Mom got home, Grandma just couldn't leave it alone. She remarked to my mother, "Holding hands with Huffy, eh?" Poor Mom was embarrassed again!

Mom and Huffy were friends into adulthood.

Mom and Huffy

Tommy

Tommy Rice was Roberta McCoy's cousin and came to visit on weekends. He was a nice boy. Mom and Tommy thought they were boyfriend and girlfriend for brief while.

Ed

The junior high school was farther from home than the elementary school had been, so the kids traveled to school by bus. Mom and a boy named Ed Preston liked each other, but were too shy to talk to each other on the bus. The school bus dropped Ed off first every evening. Once he got off the bus, he and Mom then got up the courage to talk through the bus windows and wave to each other.

Each week at the junior high school, a movie was shown. In order to support the war effort of World War II, the school sponsored a scrap iron drive. Scrap iron was highly valued and necessary in those days. It was re-used to make weapons and tools for the war effort. Everyone who wanted to see the movie had to bring enough scrap iron to buy a pass to the movie.

Unbeknownst to Mom, on one particular movie day, Ed Preston brought enough scrap iron for a pass for both of them to see the movie. Ed was saving a seat for her. No prior arrangements had been made and Mom, in her sometimes standoffish manner, went to sit with another girl. She looks back on this incident and feels bad.

Lewis

When Mom was in her later teens, she liked a handsome young man named Lewis Nelson. She would have liked to go out with him. Even though she was about eighteen, Grandpa wouldn't permit it because he felt that Lewis drove too fast. Mom respected his decision.

Wilford

Wilford Hutchinson was Ruby's brother. Wilford was a brown-haired, quiet young man. Wilford and Mom dated for a long time. He was a nice young man, but Mom just wanted to be friends.

When Mom had her appendix removed, Aunt Dorothy orchestrated having Wilford come to see her at the hospital, in an attempt to keep the ball rolling.

Wilford really liked Mom. He gave her a watch which she wore for many, many years.

When she was eighteen or nineteen, Wilford handed her a ring box and this scared her to death. When she opened it, however, it was just a beautiful birthstone ring—not an engagement ring. She was relieved. As nice as Wilford was, he was not the one Mom wanted to marry.

Neighbors and Friends

The Mullins Family

The Mullins family was pretty unforgettable. Dudalow Mullins was the **patriarch** of the family and he was just a poor pitiful country man. His wife's name was Myrt. Mom went to school with their son Rusty. Rusty had three or four little sisters. They lived in a house which had only a dirt floor. The entire family, with the exception of the youngest girl who was a very pretty little thing, chewed tobacco. Rusty vowed never to let this youngest sister chew tobacco.

After World War II began, sugar, gasoline and coffee were in short supply. According to family size, people were given rationing coupons or stamps for these items. One could only use so many coupons per week.

Schools and teachers were in charge of distributing rationing coupons. Stoney Point School had the responsibility for this process in their area. Mom and her friends Ruby, Huffy and Lewis helped distribute ration coupons and fill out paperwork after school. Mom remembers when Dudalow Mullins came to the school to get rationing books. People were required to sign their names to get their books and since Mr. Mullins couldn't read and write, he had to just make an "X".

Rationing Coupons

Sam Walters

Sam Walters was a likable, middle-aged man. He always wore overalls. He always wanted to clown around and apparently thought his attempts were brilliant. Many people, however, just thought he was silly.

When Mom was about thirteen, she and Ruby were coming home from school one day and ran into Sam. He had a message for Mom from my Grandma, asking her to borrow a "cross-eyed darning needle" from their neighbor, Ethel Maynard. Of course, there is no such thing as a "cross-eyed darning needle". Mom didn't know this, however, and did as she was told. Sam was so proud of himself for successfully pulling off this prank and he bragged about it for years to come.

Sam was drafted into the army and apparently he wasn't very happy about it. After he reported for duty, he often sat around holding a fishing pole over the ground, appearing to be "fishing on dry land". This was a **ruse** designed to convince people that he was mentally unstable, so he wouldn't have to serve in the military. Apparently this worked because the army did not keep him very long. He was discharged and drew a government pension from then on.

Sam later met a girl named Sarah Thacker who was willing to marry him - **eccentricities** and all. Sam never drove a car. After he and Sarah married, they traveled around town in a **surrey** with fringe on top. Nobody knew where he had purchased this contraption, which was a very unusual means of transportation for this area and time. He and Sarah had several boys.

John Roberts

Their neighbor, John Roberts was quite a scoundrel. He was ornery and very colorful. He hated his wife and they argued incessantly. He had a big family and drank away his pension check each month. He would steal and lie and think little of it. He was one of only four living soldiers from the Spanish-American War at that time. He had been in the cavalry and knew a lot about horses. John had a lot of spunk and people couldn't forget how, at age seventy, he was so feisty that he went and tried to enlist to serve in World War II. He was not accepted. He lived to be nearly 100 years old.

Once the shriveled up old man hired Earl and Mom to thin his corn for him. They worked all day and at the end of the day, he paid them. He paid them with a chicken. When Earl and Betty got home, they discovered that the chicken he gave to them was sick.

A day or so later, someone stole the Wiley's chickens - all of them, except for the sick one. The family was fairly certain that the chicken thief was John Roberts.

In those days, families didn't lock their doors. Crime was rare and most people could be trusted. One evening, the Wileys were all asleep when Mr. Roberts, who was drunk, stumbled into their house by mistake, assuming he was home. The noise woke up a family member, who got up, escorted John out and sent him home.

In order to get people to give him a ride, it was not unheard of for John to foolishly lay down in the middle of the road until a car came by and had to stop for him. Then he got his ride. On one occasion some neighbor boys saw him lying in the road and decided to gun their car engine. That only proved how fast John Roberts could move when he had to.

Earl

The Rock

When Mom was nine or ten years old, Grandma sent her and Earl to the store to get **kerosene** and supplies. Earl could be a challenge sometimes. On the return trip, Earl showed his brotherly love by making Mom carry everything, including the can of kerosene. As she walked along, the spigot leaked kerosene onto her leg, made her pants wet and stung her leg. Earl began to skip rocks across mud puddles in the road and splash Mom with the muddy water. Oddly enough, she tired of this after a while and asked him to stop. He wasn't quite in the mood to stop yet, so Mom sat the can down and grabbed a rock. He started to take off and even though she knew better, she threw the rock, hitting her tormenter in the back of the head. He fell into the bushes.

Mom was scared and hurried towards home. She stayed right by Grandpa's side for days in fear of Earl, until he had a chance to cool off. Earl never did claim revenge.

Earl and Mom horsing around.

Trapping and Hunting

Like most young men, when Earl was young he set traps to catch rabbits or groundhogs to eat. Mom, however, loved animals. She often went with him and knew where his traps were set. Not being aware of how difficult it would be for injured animals to fend for themselves, she often innocently went to his traps and released the trapped animals, thinking she was doing them a favor. Earl never appeared to catch on to this fact and was never told about it until he was old.

Mom sometimes went with Earl when he hunted squirrels. Naturally, it's important to be quiet when hunting. Mom often made noise or talked too much and Earl became annoyed. He had to make her be quiet so she wouldn't scare the squirrels away.

The Runaway

Earl had always been rather strong-willed and hard-headed. One morning when he was approximately fifteen years old, he was thoroughly enjoying sleeping in, when Grandma woke him up. He hadn't had quite enough beauty rest yet and was very angry about being awakened. He was so angry, in fact, that he made the poor decision to run away and he roamed the country for about a week. He hopped freight trains from place to place and was finally arrested as a runaway. Earl was jailed in Kenova, West Virginia, the home of Grandma's brother, Jonah Adkins. As Earl looked out of the jail window, he saw his uncle and yelled to him. Jonah helped him. Earl was transferred to the Wayne County jail for a couple more days and then he was released.

The Lamps

Poverty was never far from the Wiley's minds, but through it all they were pretty content. Earl always enjoyed telling stories. The family only owned two kerosene lamps at that time - a rather pitiful supply of lighting. One of the instances he enjoyed recalling was when one of the family members accidentally dropped one lamp onto the other and both lamps broke. This is sort of like the phrase "If it weren't for bad luck, we'd have no luck at all." The family became good at laughing at themselves and their circumstances.

The Belt

Punishment at the Wiley home was often "by the belt". For obvious reasons, Earl was disciplined pretty regularly. Sometimes Grandma ran in between Grandpa and Uncle Earl when punishment was due. She just couldn't bear to see it or to have Earl hurt.

Crime and Punishment

One evening Bill and Mom went up the road to get milk from their neighbors. The neighbors had an only child named Josephine. She wanted them to stay longer to talk, so they did. They didn't feel that they were doing anything wrong but they stayed too late.

When they got home, Grandpa was furious. He hit Mom with his belt. Mom was seldom rebellious like Uncle Earl and Aunt Dorothy, but this was an exception. After Grandpa hit her, he asked her if she was ever going to stay late again. She replied that she would whenever she took the notion. Grandpa told her that she was just as stubborn as Aunt Dorothy.

*

When Uncle Bill was fifteen or sixteen, he went with friends into Huntington, approximately twelve miles from home. Bill wanted to see a movie, but his friends wanted to do something else. They arranged to pick him up after the movie.

Unfortunately, they didn't come back. Huntington had curfew laws and Bill was afraid to stick around, so he started walking home.

Grandma began to wonder where her baby was and as the hours ticked by, she became more and more agitated. She started to scream and cry and the crying eventually woke up Mom. Grandpa must have been away and Mom went to get Louise's husband, Walter, to help them. The three of them got into the car and headed toward Huntington, with Grandma still crying and carrying on the whole way.

Finally, as they neared Huntington, the headlights illuminated a young figure walking toward them. It was Bill!

Grandma grabbed him and hugged him. She looked him over and when she saw that he was all right, she whipped him.

Leisure

Leisure time was spent in a variety of ways. Church was very important to this community and people generally attended three times per week; Sunday morning, Sunday evening, and Wednesday night. The people enjoyed worship services. The Wileys lived a couple of miles from the church and walked to and from services. The young people had great fun walking to and from church, much like they did walking to and from school. Mom remembers that warm summer air and how much the young people enjoyed these journeys.

There was always a large crowd coming from church after services. A man named Penny Thacker was usually with the group and often, as they progressed down the road, someone asked him to dance. Everyone stopped on the little-traveled road and Penny shouted the silly phrase, "Jolly Susan, hit the floor!" Then, with one hand behind his back, he danced to entertain them. He was a great dancer and everybody enjoyed watching him.

Sometimes the Sunday School teachers had parties at their homes and invited the children to come. The church had potluck dinners and ice cream socials and was an important social network of the community. For Christmas, the church gave each child who attended a bag of treats.

For fun, Louise or Dorothy would sometimes have parties at home to celebrate birthdays or other occasions.

There was an occasion where personalities from radio station WSAZ in Huntington were in the vicinity and asked the school teacher at Stoney Point if they could entertain at the school. Churches and schools occasionally had shows which helped to raise small amounts of money and the teacher agreed.

Everyone came to the show and paid admission. People came who never went anywhere else. The name of one of the radio personalities was Ray Myers and he had been born without arms. A steel guitar was laid on the floor and he managed somehow to chord and play the guitar with his feet. The lead singers were Slim and Tex. They played the guitar and sang. Natchee the Indian played the fiddle. Everybody had a good time. The event raised a small sum for playground equipment - not the kind we think of now days - just balls, bats, games and jump ropes.

Grandma asked the kids not to stay up late and waste their kerosene supply. Bedtime was early. Sometimes they laid and talked until they became sleepy. Earl took a flashlight to bed with him and enjoyed playing with it. Every morning the family got up before daylight.

During the night, they used a lantern to find their way to the outhouse. At other times, especially on cold winter evenings, a bucket was brought into the house to serve as a chamber pot.

Louise and Dorothy loved making quilts. Their two favorite patterns were the double wedding ring and the Dutch girl. Mom didn't have as much material to work with as her sisters did, so she just made little quilts. The girls also liked to **embroider**.

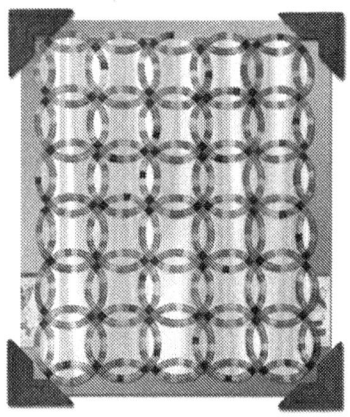

A Double Wedding Ring Quilt

Farmers in the area raised **sugar cane**. At harvest time, a man who owned heavy cane processing machinery traveled from farm to farm with his equipment and a small crew. This machinery was set up in the middle of the sugar cane field to process the sugar cane. This provided an opportunity for a party. Young people came from all around the area and a large crowd gathered. The sugar cane was cut, piled, ground and made into molasses. The syrup ran down a trough into containers. A bonfire was built. Everyone got delicious samples of the molasses. It was a fun social gathering and often they had entertainment. Morris Frazier, who was the cousin of a neighbor, was a very talented guitar player. He was a good singer as well, and everyone enjoyed the entertainment. He often came from Ohio to visit and he provided a pleasant diversion at community gatherings.

At home, Grandma had lady visitors during the day. In the evenings, Grandpa's friends came to visit. Grandpa was a great storyteller and always kept people entertained. The men enjoyed talking with each other.

The family enjoyed sitting around the fireplace. They often roasted small potatoes in the skins, in the red hot coals of fire. They also popped popcorn over the fire.

They enjoyed listening to radio broadcasts. One of their favorites was "The Shadow", which was a mystery detective-type radio story. Shouts of "Hi-Ho Silver," and "Who was that masked man?" could be heard, as they listened to "The Lone Ranger". They also listened to "Superman," "Dagwood and Blondie" and "Jack Benny". On Saturday evenings, they enjoyed hearing the music of "The Grand Old Opry". They listened to some romantic soap operas, which weren't racy like modern soap operas are.

Grandpa loved listening to the major league baseball games and prize fights (boxing) on the radio. This was during the heyday of the legendary boxer, Jack Dempsey.

Louise and Mom liked to play dolls together. Mom liked to read.

Family members also liked playing their version of "I Spy", where someone spotted something in the room that was of a certain color or shape, and others got to guess what that object was.

They enjoyed playing checkers. Mom, Uncle Bill, Grandpa and Aunt Louise liked to play cards. Their favorite game was 500 Rummy.

Mom and Aunt Louise cut out people's pictures and clothing from the Spiegel and Montgomery Ward catalogs they received. In this manner, they created paper dolls to play with, as well as boyfriends for the dolls they had made. Of course, they were able to change the doll's clothing as they wished. It was part of the process in those days of making your own fun. Mom says she wouldn't change any of these experiences even if she could. It was an **idyllic** time.

This and That

When Uncle Bill was about ten, he loved to tie a towel or rag around his neck like a cape and jump from rocks and pretend he was Superman or Batman. On one such occasion, he asked Huffy Stevens to play the game with him. Huffy played, but then he went to tell the other kids in the community about it. It didn't take long for word to spread and once it did, other children enjoyed teasing Bill about his fantasies.

*

Aunt Dorothy married a man named Bill Rush. Bill served in the army during World War II in France and Germany. Once when he came home on leave, he brought my Uncle Bill an army dress cap. Uncle Bill was very proud of that cap and wore it all the time. It was his prized possession.

Dorothy and Bill Rush

Bill (wearing his Army cap), Mom, and their nephew Donnie.

When Bill was about ten years old, he saw an ad in a comic book and ordered a Charles Atlas Body Building Kit. Charles Atlas was a famous body builder - the Arnold Schwarzeneggar of that day. Uncle Bill wanted to grow up to become big and muscular. When his body building kit arrived, this gave his brother and sisters yet another reason to pick on Bill and make sport of him.

*

The Wileys raised chickens. Of course, some of the baby chicks died before they grew up. Earl, Bill and Mom did the proper thing and put the little dead chicks in country match boxes, conducted chicken funerals and then buried them.

They didn't have a garden hose to play with. Instead, the children drew water from their well and filled several tubs with water. They allowed the water to warm in the sun and then threw the water over each other for summer fun.

*

When Mom and Bill were little, toys were scarce, so they improvised. They made pretend cars out of match boxes or blocks of wood. They dug and carved roads out of the hillsides and ran their cars over the roads they had made.

*

They had "rooster fights", using violets from the yard. Each would grab a violet, hook their bloom around the other's bloom and jerk. The one who pulled the bloom from the other's stem was the winner.

*

They also learned to hold a blade of grass between the thumbs of both hands and blow through it to create the perfect whistle or noisemaker.

*

When Mom was in school, they bought their school books. She usually bought them used in order to save some money. When she became a bit older, she couldn't find a used math book to buy. She had seen what the new ones looked like. They were bright orange and very nice, and she was looking forward to having one. She was going to be so proud of it. She asked Grandpa to buy her the new math book and he agreed. Grandpa went to buy the book. Unfortunately, there were some times when Grandpa drank more than he should have and this was one of those times. After he purchased the book and headed home, he navigated across a swinging foot bridge. He didn't navigate too well, however, for he and the book both fell into the creek. He brought the soggy, waterlogged book home, and eventually it dried out so that it could be used. Mom was extremely disappointed.

Mom and Bill have always been close. They used to like to tease each other and fight. Mom often used to come up behind Bill in a very sly and subtle manner and pinch or poke him. Bill, however, was not subtle in his response. He would haul off and openly hit her. Of course Bill is the one my Grandpa saw acting badly. Grandpa must have thought Bill was some sort of a maniac hitting seemingly-sweet, innocent little Betty. Bill got whipped and Betty went on her merry way.

*

When Mom was a teenager, she asked Grandpa to cut a Christmas tree. He did so, but he came back with the ugliest, most crooked tree anyone has ever seen. Normally, the kids were never bossy or demanding of their father. Doing so was not a good idea. But in this case Mom told him if she couldn't have a nice straight Christmas tree she didn't want one at all. Grandpa didn't say a word, but meekly went out and cut another one for her.

*

When Earl was about sixteen years old, he participated in the CCC (Civilian Conservation Corps). This was a government sponsored make-work program designed to provide employment opportunities for young men. President Franklin Roosevelt wanted to prevent soil **erosion**, save the land and provide employment to young, unemployed men after the Great Depression hit the United States. These young men performed various tasks. They built roads, bridges and fire towers, fought fires, performed erosion control work, restored historical sites and planted trees. Earl and his friend, Denver McCoy went to Idaho to work during their stint with the CCC. The young men were fed by the CCC and were paid approximately $30.00 per month for their services.

*

When Mom was about thirteen, (and old enough to know better) she and Uncle Bill were having breakfast at the kitchen table. A family friend named Sam Walters was visiting and Grandma had gone outside to care for the chickens and the cow. Mom and Bill began comparing the amounts of milk in their glasses. One accused the other of having more milk in their glass than the other. This highly important argument escalated until the table was turned over and everything was broken. Sam thought the incident was rather funny, but Grandma did not.

Uncle Bill made the decision to go and enlist in the National Guard when he was about fourteen years old. He appeared to be about eighteen years old at the time and wasn't questioned about it. In those days, my grandmother didn't have a clue as to what the National Guard was. She just thought it was someplace to go every Tuesday night. It was Aunt Dorothy's husband, Bill Rush, who warned Grandma to get Bill out of the Guard and explained the possibility of war duties to her. Uncle Bill was "sprung" from duty.

Uncle Bill later served in the Korean War

Bill in his National Guard Uniform

Bill's dog tags and uniform buttons from the Korean War

Baltimore

Aunt Louise married a man named Walter Gillum. He got a job working in the ship yards in Baltimore, Maryland during World War II, prior to his military service. Louise and Walter moved to Baltimore. Eventually Uncle Earl and Grandpa also got jobs at the ship yards where they built and worked on ships. They traveled back and forth from their home to Baltimore.

When Mom was about thirteen, Aunt Louise became pregnant with her first child and she invited Mom to come and visit her in Baltimore. Uncle Earl took Mom to Baltimore on the train. Traveling by train was a lot of fun. As the train crossed the **Mason-Dixon Line** over into Virginia, Mom caught her first glimpse of **segregation**. At this point, the conductor asked all the blacks on the train to move to another car. No questions were asked. They just moved. Unfortunately, discrimination was a way of life in those days.

This was one of many trips Mom took by train. Mom loved being on the trains.

Earl and his car

Reflections

By 1946, all five of the children gravitated to Columbus, Ohio, with Aunt Dorothy leading the way. The older three were married by now. Bill and Betty lived with Grandpa and Grandma until they each married. Things were different, but yet they were the same.

On one occasion, Bill was taking a nap, when Mom thought it would be cute to tie his big toe to the foot of the bed. He woke up, tried to get out of bed and found that he couldn't get out. Then the screaming started. Grandma came to the rescue and helped Uncle Bill untie himself. There wasn't much doubt about who the perpetrator was. Bill knew who had done it. He was used to it by now.

*

My grandparents passed away when I was a teenager. Years passed and I was close to twenty years old. Uncle Earl, Aunt Dorothy, Uncle Bill and their families, Mom, Dad and I traveled to Beckley, West Virginia for the funeral of my great uncle Tom, one of Grandpa's brothers.

Tom's home was beautiful, with a huge front porch and it lay just a short distance up on a hill from his church, where the funeral was held. Tom was a fine craftsman and one of his talents was stained glass work. He had installed all new stained glass windows in the church. They were so beautiful. They are a part of his legacy - and ours.

*

The beauty and serenity of the area was awesome. I could hear the unique names from the past echoing. Flem Stanley, Ivory Lee Staley, Fuzzy Mills and all of the others - the rural names which sound so strange today. The word "wasper", comes to mind and makes me smile. This was a word our family used to identify the insect commonly known as the wasp. How charming the word now seems. Those surroundings helped me understand and appreciate what a wonderful opportunity my family had to grow up poor in the back woods of West Virginia, deprived of really nothing that was truly important and blessed with everything that they really needed.

Got stories?

What was life like for your family growing up in a place and time far removed from today? You, too, may have stories of an earlier America when life was simpler. Before they are forgotten, would you like to share these adventures with generations who may otherwise never know? We can't promise that we will have the time to personally respond to each email, but we'd still love to hear from you!

Contact us at **SnapshotsStories@hotmail.com**

Student Glossary

Al Capone: a famous gangster who ran a crime ring in Chicago in the 1920's and early 1930's; was arrested for not paying taxes

Brilliantine: an oily substance used in the hair to make it shiny

Chaste: pure

Depression: a period of economic crisis and unemployment caused by the huge 1929 Stock Market Crash

Eccentricities: strange things about a person or place

Embroider: to decorate with stitching or needlework

Erosions: areas where dirt or rocks have been worn away by wind or rain

Foyer: lobby or entrance

Hearth: the front or bottom of a fireplace

Ice Box: an early type of refrigerator; basically a box which held blocks of ice and any food items

Idyllic: charming, simple, ideal

Kerosene: a thin fuel used for heat or light

Knickers: loose-fitting, baggy pants that go down to the knees

Mason-Dixon Line: an invisible geographic line that separated Southern states from Northern states; considered the division between free states and states that still had slaves

Outhouse: a restroom located outdoors in a small building

Patriarch: male leader or eldest member of a family

Rouge: red or pink cosmetics for the cheeks; blush

Ruse: a trick

Sassafras Tea: tea made using the bark from the root of Sassafras trees

Segregation: keeping public areas for white people separate from public areas for black people

Shipyards: areas where ships are built or repaired

Smokehouse: a small building where meat was prepared using smoke

Stock Market Crash: a sudden drop in stock prices

Sugar Cane: tall grass-like plant with sap that contains sugar

Surrey: a four-wheeled horse-drawn carriage

Washboard: a rough, rectangular board or surface that dirty laundry was rubbed across to get it clean

Ideas for Educators

Discussion

• In the 30's and 40's many families were too poor to buy toys for their children. Instead, the children would often make up games or use items they had around the house as toys. In this book, we read about the paper dolls that the girls used to make by cutting out pictures of people and clothing from catalogs. Bill also used to use a towel or rag as a "cape" and pretend he was a super hero. The children also liked to pretend that match boxes were cars. Do your students think that they are better off today with all the toys and products they have or do they think that the children in the stories were better off getting to make up their own fun? Have the students discuss the differences between the children in the stories and the children of today. Have them discuss the similarities between the two eras. What fun games, toys, or projects can the students come up with that don't involve commercial items or toys? Is it really such a bad thing to be poor? What other things in life are more important than money and belongings?

• Charlie was part of a family that consisted of thirteen children and two parents. How many people are in the students' families? Do the students think that it would be better to have a large family or a small one? What were the advantages of having a large family in the past? What are the advantages now? What were the disadvantages of having a large family in the time period discussed in the book? What are the disadvantages now?

Essay

• The stories in this book are true ones – tales shared between the generations. Have your students get involved in their own story-sharing project. Students could write about a happy or memorable experience that one of their grandparents or older neighbors had when he/she was a child. Make sure that each student sets aside a significant period of time to really talk to this older person and to learn from them. Have them record as much detail about the story as possible. Do the students have a similar experience from their own lives that they would like to share?

• Segregation was a part of everyday life in many places in the 1930's and 1940's. There was separate housing and separate public facilities for African Americans and there were many times when whites refused to serve blacks at restaurants or to even let black children attend school with white children. In this book, we read about an instance where Betty was on a train and witnessed segregation first hand for the first time in her life. Blacks were asked to move to their own separate train car. How would the children feel if they witnessed something like this today? How would they feel if they were asked to move to a different seat just because of their race, sex, looks, or religion?

Activity

• The holidays were always a fun time for the families in this book. Many celebrations were held in the communities. Betty and her friends dressed up for Halloween and made Christmas decorations. They had Easter egg hunts, plays, and holiday-related games. Have the students get involved with an activity that the children in this book also participated in. Students could string popcorn or wrap pine cones in aluminum foil to make Christmas ornaments or have a Halloween costume contest. Use the name of the holiday or words associated with the holiday as anagrams like the teacher did in the story we read about. Whatever activity your students do, make sure it relates to the stories they read about here and have them discuss or write about what they do to celebrate holidays at their homes. Do they do some of the same things that the children in this book did?

• This book tells the stories of a family in rural West Virginia and Kentucky in the 1930's and 1940's. The family mostly lived in small towns along the border between the two states. Have the students find this general area on a recent map of the United States. Can they find all of the towns that are talked about in the stories they have read? What other information can they find about these towns today? What are the local populations of these towns in current times? When were these towns established and what were their populations and industries in the 30's and 40's? Have the children use as many resources as possible (maps/atlases, the internet, almanacs, town charters, local newspapers, guidebooks, etc) to get an idea of what these towns were like when they first appeared, what they were like during the times outlined in this book, and what they are like today.

Critical Thinking

• During World War II, American citizens had to do without many items so that there would be enough supplies for the troops. One part of this book deals with the rationing stamps which people received and redeemed for goods. Some of the items that were frequently rationed out included sugar, gas, nylon, rubber, meat, aluminum, butter, shoes, silk, and coffee. What would the lives of your students be like if they had to give up these items? What products might they have to do without? How much harder would life be for them and their families? Americans were also encouraged to collect rubber, metal, and paper. The children in this book also often participated in scrap metal drives (including drives which offered the reward of a movie). How were these drives similar to the recycling programs of today? How are they different? What war items might have been made using the rationed goods? Are any of the children involved in any sort of recycling program at home or school? What could the items they recycle be made into one day? What are some good reasons to recycle in today's world?

www.ingramcontent.com/pod-product-compliance
Lightning Source LLC
Chambersburg PA
CBHW031415040426
42444CB00005B/575